# INVESTING SIMPLIFIED

*Building Wealth One Step at a Time*

B. VINCENT

QuantumQuill Press

# CONTENTS

1 Introduction 1
2 Getting Started with Investing 2
3 Types of Investments 8
4 Investing Strategies 13
5 Risk Management 19
6 Retirement Planning 25
7 Tax Considerations 30
8 Monitoring and Adjusting Your Portfolio 35

Copyright © 2024 by B. Vincent

All rights reserved. No part of this book may be reproduced in any manner whatsoever without written permission except in the case of brief quotations embodied in critical articles and reviews.

First Printing, 2024

# CHAPTER 1

# Introduction

An all too common experience for individual investors with a substantial investment is one of significant confusion. Everyone has a 'hot tip', but the problem is that the 'tips' usually conflict. A study of some of the stocks recommended as a 'buy' and a comparison to the same analyst's 'sells' on other stocks might be enlightening. Even advice from industry professionals such as brokers can be conflicting. There are many reasons for this, but the simple fact is that successful investing is extremely difficult and complex for professionals, let alone amateurs. A simpler approach is more likely to work well.

Investing doesn't have to be complicated to be effective. Following simple and straightforward principles may significantly improve your success at investment. 'Investing Simplified' may help you achieve the elusive goal of meaningful returns on your investment. At the same time, it might help you to sleep better even in the midst of today's troubled times. You should be prepared to spend time on this. Many of the principles are simple, but you may need time to let them sink in. This may very well be the most important time you have ever spent, as measured by return on time invested.

# CHAPTER 2

# Getting Started with Investing

Keep in mind that you do not want to take too much risk or too little risk, and you want to avoid investing in a level of risk that will cause you financial distress. Different types of investment can be split between different risk and return levels. The most effective investment strategy is to diversify your investment across different types of assets according to your risk and return. A practical understanding of risk, risk and return, and liquidity will also aid your selection of investments.

Liquidity: A liquid investment can be readily converted into cash with little loss of capital and it is normally associated with low levels of risk. High levels of liquidity usually involve an investment in cash or cash equivalent. At the other end of the scale, an investment in buildings or other fixed assets is low in liquidity because it takes time to sell the asset and the seller may have to accept a lower price in order to offload the asset. It is important to weigh up the liquidity of an investment against both the level of risk and the returns expected.

Risk tolerance: how much can you afford to lose? All investments involve taking on risk. It is helpful to think in terms of risk and return. Low levels of risk are associated with low potential returns but also low potential loss. Higher levels of risk are associated with high potential return but also high potential loss. Usually, the riskier an investment, the higher the potential returns but also the higher the potential losses.

Understand why you are investing. Before you start investing, it is important to understand why you are investing. Your purpose will determine how you approach investment as well as the level of risk that you take on. Different types of investment carry different levels of risk, return, and liquidity. Defining your risk tolerance and investment will determine which types of investment are more suitable for you.

## 2.1. Setting Financial Goals

Throughout this process, it is important to talk it over with your spouse or your financial partner. You need to be setting these goals together. Make sure you write down your goals. This will make them more "concrete". Without a firm idea of what your goals are and when you will need to achieve them, it will be very difficult to determine how much risk you will need to take and how to choose the appropriate investments. Always keep in mind that your goal is to choose investments that will earn a specific rate of return in order to achieve your goals. For example, Cathy needs $120,000 to pay for her 2 children's college tuition in 10 years. She will be looking for an investment that will earn an average of 8-10% during that time frame.

Next, you need to set a long-term goal. Usually, this will be retirement. Calculate how much money you will need to sustain your desired lifestyle when you retire, and when you would like to retire. Keep in mind that nowadays, the future of Social Security is uncertain, and it is very likely that it will be a non-factor for the younger generations. Chances are you will need to be fully responsible for your own retirement and will need to factor this into your planning. By setting a concrete goal now, you will be in a better position to take the appropriate amount of risk to achieve your goal.

The first thing you need to do before you start is "getting started". You would not believe how easy it is to bypass this basic step, but circumstances change. Our goals change based on our changing needs, and they are the measures we will use to tell how well we are doing in the future. Start by setting a short-term goal. Do you need to establish an emergency fund? If so, how much do you need to put away? For example, you may need to put away $5,000 in the next year. You have a specific goal with a specific time limit. Or you may want to buy a home. You will need a down payment. How much will you need? Set a time limit. This kind of goal will help determine how much risk you will need to take with your investment.

*2.2. Understanding Risk and Return*

The levels of risk are usually defined by their standard deviation. This is a statistical measure of the historic volatility of a given investment. Each investor must evaluate their risk tolerance when choosing investments. A risk-averse person is likely to steer clear from high-risk, high-return investments that a more aggressive investor would find suitable. An older person with impending retirement may be in need of a low-risk, low-return investment, whereas someone in the early stages of their career may be in need of a high-risk, high-return investment. It is crucial that you match your risk and return objectives when developing an investment plan. High-risk investments should not be funded at the expense of the higher returns, jeopardizing the financial future of the investor or his ability to reach his financial goals.

Understanding the relationship between risk and return is crucial to successful investing. Safest investments, like government bonds, offer a low return. Higher returns are associated with higher risk. For example, investing in micro cap stocks carries a higher risk of a greater loss, but also the possibility of a greater gain, than investing in a large cap blue chip stock. Usually time horizon is used to divide investment between speculation and the long term investment. Short time periods are generally for speculation, which is more akin to gambling than actual investing. This does not mean that you cannot use a long term investment strategy on high risk investments. It only means that you must take into consideration the higher probability of short term loss, before investing money that you will need for a large purchase or a comfortable retirement.

## 2.3. Creating an Investment Plan

What is your risk tolerance? This is how you would feel if your investment portfolio fluctuated in value. Would you lose it? Would you be unable to achieve your goal? Would you lose sleep? Different investments have different risk levels. A single stock can provide high returns but lose more of its value than the entire stock market during a recession. A US savings bond has very low risk; however, the returns on the investment are also very low. Your risk tolerance and the investment time horizon are related. The more time you have before a goal, the more risk you can take because there is more time to recover from a loss. An old rule of thumb says that your risk tolerance should be 100 minus your age so that at retirement age, your investment portfolio should reflect it. However, investments vary greatly in potential returns and risk, as do people in the same age group. So it is questionable whether this is a good rule.

What is your time horizon? This is the period of time in which you would like to achieve your financial goal. If your goal is to send a kid to private school, your time horizon is sometime between the ages of 5 and 18. If your goal is to retire at age 55, your time horizon is the number of years until age 55. If your time horizon is short, there may be a limit to the types of investments you can make due to tax considerations. For example, the tax on a CD is just too high for the investment to be worth it.

What are my investment goals? Do I want to retire early and take a world cruise? Do I want to send my kids to private school and pay for their college? Do I want to start my own business or buy my dream home? Your investment goals will depend on who you are and what your aspirations are.

A good investment plan should identify (in writing) your investment goals, time frames, your starting point, and your risk tolerance. It should spell out the strategies you will use to meet your goals. It should also include a detailed account of your investment portfolio. Your investment plan is really a roadmap that should lead you to your investment goals. The plan begins with asking a lot of questions. The following are questions you should ask yourself.

*2.4. Choosing the Right Investment Account*

Once these points are determined, a suitable investment account becomes more obvious. If the education funds are for young children, an account where the owner maintains control until a certain future date, but the assets are in an account for which earnings and capital gains are not taxed, with relatively low risk on the principal, would be the best option. This is due to the tax advantages and the ability to ensure that funds are available, and if some are lost due to an investment decline, the difference is replaced from other savings. This type of an account is best provided by a specific type of 529 plan account or custodial Roth IRA. If retirement income is the goal for an account with the current income beneficiary as the future owner, the best account will usually be a trust of same nature as in the previous example, provided that the cost for the trust is worth the account gains and the trustee can perform a complete investment plan for the account. With such a trust there is still another option to act as the future income and account owner, creating a trust with less investment directives and simply naming the future income beneficiary as the trustee. The other possibilities for account owners and their investment instructions can be easily deduced from the mentioned examples.

Important factors to consider in choosing the right investment account include: 1) the purpose for the account, 2) who will own the account, 3) availability of withdrawals, and 4) who will provide investment instructions. The purpose for the account leads to an examination of ownership and control. If the funds are for a child's education, the account will have a different purpose than an account to save for a second home. If the money is to finance a future or current income need and the account owner is nearing or in retirement, studies suggest that the person owning the account should be the same as the person for whom the money is being invested, in both of these cases. This is because in the event of death or incapacitation of the account owner, funds would likely be needed or desired by the future income beneficiary, and thus ownership by the same person as the intended future income beneficiary simplifies and reduces the cost of managing the transfer of account assets.

## 2.5. Building an Emergency Fund

The purpose of an emergency fund is fundamentally to act as a cash fund in an emergency situation. Consider any potential occurrence that would prevent your capacity to attend work regularly or perhaps the loss of a job. These situations could require funding in the form of short-term insurance, in the event of a gap between jobs, or in a worst-case situation, an alternative to gainful employment may have to be sought. This is precisely what an emergency fund caters for. By temporarily suspending investment of current savings funds, an event such as this could be weathered without any negative long-term impact.

The most striking aspect of arguing the case for establishing an emergency fund was the uncertainty of life.

An emergency fund represents a crucial component of wealth management. Established properly, emergency funds can prevent the depression of high-interest debt, bankruptcy, and eviction.

# CHAPTER 3

# Types of Investments

Stocks are equity investments in a company. When ownership of a stock is purchased, the owner becomes a shareholder of a company. Stocks have the potential for large returns in the short to medium term. It's these potential returns that drive the increase in risk. Although stock investors are passengers on a life-threatening roller coaster, it's one which can provide and/or destroy great wealth. Decide when you're willing to get off.

When investing in securities or the markets, there are many ways to skin a cat, and you will be bombarded with a wide variety of investment options. Generally, these options fall under one or more of the main asset classes. Each investment has its own set of characteristics, rewards, and risks. Most investors will stick to the asset class with which they're most familiar. This makes sense as there's enough learning to do in this one area before exploring and diversifying into others.

*3.1. Stocks*

Stocks are shares of ownership in a company. Owning stock gives the owner certain rights within the company. Often, when we look at investing in stocks, we are looking towards the future and the security of our resources. Investors choose stocks for many reasons, and many times the best investment is to set aside a sum of money that won't be diversity in the form of a sector rotation strategy using relatively low-cost ETFs, the risk and return can be optimized compared to a strategy with less diversity.

Sector ETFs and specific style ETFs would be considered the satellite principle which involves taking on additional risk to achieve a higher return. An investor who seeks to use a global strategy can do the same by dividing investments in international or regional index ETFs at a higher performance ratio than switching between ADRs of different countries and buying and selling international funds.

Now an equity investor can have similar core and satellite strategies with an even better performance ratio using exchange traded funds. These funds offer diversity equivalent or better than index funds while also allowing for the use of market timing and sector rotation strategies. The investor could invest a small portion in an S&P 500 ETF as a core strategy and use the rest as well as future investments in times of a strong market to buy more sector-specific ETFs or even small cap style-specific ETFs while still achieving an overall performance higher than 11%.

By comparing it to a computer processor's ability, AG Edwards chief investment strategist Sam Stovall noted that the S&P 500, which is a fair market proxy for big cap stocks, has about an 11% performance ratio. Meanwhile, the S&P Small Cap 600 Growth Index is a good proxy for small cap product and service stocks, which comprise the industry groups of the current example. The S&P 600 has had about a 20% performance ratio. These figures assume the investor had invested in those stocks directly.

*3.5. Real Estate*

Real estate is an investment in property consisting of land and the buildings on it, together with its natural resources such as minerals, water, and flora. It is immovable property of this nature; an interest vested in this an item of real property, buildings, or housing in general. However, there are some people who are truly connected with real estate investment. Why? This is because real estate is a solid investment. The value of real estate can change and, in principle, goes up. If the property is well located, maintained well, and has a good environment, then the value will surely appreciate. We can see this from the price of land, buildings, up to luxurious homes continuing to improve. That is why many investors turn to set up their investment in real estate. But even so, there are also incalculable risks in this investment. Prices can vary depending on certain conditions. If prices are going down when we want to sell it, this will be a loss for us. In addition, the monthly costs will also go out to maintain the property, ranging from renovation, tax, cost of borrowing, etc. High costs and high leverage can be very profitable if we invest in property to rent, where the rent money can cover the entire cost, and if lucky, we still have a surplus. And for the investors who have this type of property, if the property location is accessible and strategic, it can be converted into a quite promising student's boarders.

# CHAPTER 4

# Investing Strategies

One of the greatest proponents of this strategy is Warren Buffett, the greatest investor of all time. As opposed to high frequency traders, he says the best approach to building wealth is to buy and hold a broad-based, low-cost index fund. Index funds are suitable for a buy and hold strategy as they have low turnover and are tax efficient. With a long-term horizon of ten years or more, it is likely you will see the value of your investment double. Also, buying and holding onto blue chip stocks that pay out dividends is very effective. In time, the dividends themselves could well be sending you a nice check.

This is a strategy advocated by the majority of investment advisors. The idea of this strategy is very simple: if you have selected the right investments, the best approach is to hold onto your investments through good times and bad. Eventually, the theory is, you will be able to gain profit, although it is likely to take several years.

*4.1. Buy and Hold Strategy*

One of the oft-cited reasons for B and H's superiority is that it's more tax-efficient. This is due to the rate of taxation for long-term capital gains, which the government loves to change now and then, but regardless, it's usually much lower than the rate for short-term gains.

This is an advantage shared by value investors, who see quality stocks at low prices as long-term capital gains opportunities.

A short-term trader will frequently pay so much attention to the macroeconomic environment and changes to specific sectors and industries that they will poorly diversify, i.e., they'll buy a bunch of companies in an industry they think is going to do fine and ignore industries that are out of favor. This is quite the opposite of the person who wants to buy and hold shares of a high-quality diversified mix of stocks. Periods of indiscriminate selling provide the B and H investor with a smorgasbord of opportunities to pick up quality stocks, often at amazingly low prices. In the end, a B and H investor is actually rooting for a bear market, knowing that if they can get in cheap now, it will mean big profits when the market turns around.

Consider a long-term investment strategy, which involves buying and holding a portfolio of investments, and it is known as the "Buy and Hold" strategy. B and H adherents don't worry too much about various market swings. Short-term volatility is a foe for many strategies, as it creates an unclear picture of the changes occurring within a company. As a result, the short-term trader, looking for a profit based on the market reacting to a company's changes, frequently buys into a company that is actually showing a downturn. Consequently, the B and H investor feels that short-term volatility is their ally because the increased level of wrong decisions regarding the purchase or sale of individual stocks provides a greater opportunity to buy low.

*4.2. Dollar-Cost Averaging*

The bonus to investing using dollar cost averaging is that it forces you to invest more into an investment when the price is low, which is the exact time that you should be investing more. This of course is counter-intuitive to most investors, and in effect greedy investors will do the exact opposite and put more money into an investment after it has risen, since they feel that it is a good investment, and they want to get more out of it. Since this is opposite to what should be done it leads to investors buying high and selling low, the exact opposite of a sound investment strategy.

Using this technique, you'll end up buying more shares of an investment when its price is low and fewer shares when its price is high. You'll also find yourself not caring about the price of the investment, because you know that it would still be a good price since you are buying fewer shares when the price is high, and more shares when the price is low. Over time, you'll effectively lower the average price per share. This technique of effectively lowering the average price of a share is what dollar-cost averaging is all about.

With dollar-cost averaging, you don't need to worry about whether or not today is the right time to buy a particular investment. You are simply trying to invest some amount of money every month, week or quarter — for example $100. The investment can be split among a few stocks or a stock and a mutual fund. The point is that you have a set amount of money to invest, and you put it to work on a regular basis.

When you don't have a lump sum to invest, one of the hardest parts of investing is deciding when to buy a stock or mutual fund. You may be concerned that today's a good time to buy, but what if prices drop in the future? You don't want to buy an investment only to see its price drop and your money disappear. One way around this is by using a technique called dollar-cost averaging.

*4.3. Value Investing*

One key metric for a value investor is the P/E ratio of a company. This can be found by taking the current stock price of the company and dividing it by the company's Earnings per Share (EPS). This ratio provides a look at what the market is willing to pay for the company's earnings. The higher the P/E ratio, the more the market is willing to pay. EPS is a reflection of a company's profitability. Value investors will generally target stocks with high EPS and low P/E ratios. This usually indicates that the stock is currently undervalued. Many value investors also target the price-to-book ratio of a stock. This ratio provides a comparison between a company's book value and its current market price.

Prices under a book value indicate that the company is selling for less than its worth.

Value investing is one of the most well-known stock-picking methods. The goal is to uncover stocks that are trading at a price lower than their true worth. There are two ways to make money on a value stock. The first is when the stock price comes up to reflect the worth of the company. If the stock is purchased at a significant discount, there is potential for a large profit. If a stock is purchased at fair value Price-to-Earnings ratio (P/E) of 10, and the stock price doubles, the investor has made a 100% return. The second way to make money with value stocks is through dividends. Companies that pay dividends generally do so because they have reached a stable point in their growth. If a company has good potential for growth, a value investor could receive great returns if the stock price goes up to reflect the worth. High yields can be very profitable because the investor can then reinvest the dividends into more stock at the same high rate.

*4.4. Growth Investing*

When you purchase a growth stock, you are buying a share in a company that you believe has outstanding potential for growth. The goal is to purchase a growth stock and sell it at some future date for a substantial profit. Most shares of all small companies and startup companies are issued to raise capital to develop the company. When a company issues shares that are growth stocks, it usually means that the company will take the capital and reinvest it into the company to further its development. These companies will use the capital to expand their research and development division, make new products, or expand into a new market. The ultimate goal here is to increase the value of the company so that its share price will rise and the company can issue more shares at a higher price. Growth stocks will not pay a high dividend, if any at all. It will be unlikely to find a growth stock that has a long history of paying high dividends because these companies want to reinvest their earnings back into the company. Step one to deciding whether a growth stock is right for you is to look at your personal objectives and risk tolerance. Due to the fact that growth stocks are on the lower end of the risk/reward ratio, it is important to assess how well this stock will help you to achieve your objectives. If you are saving for a long-term goal, such as retirement or a college fund, growth stocks will be a suitable option due to the capital gains. If you are in need of income or are saving for a short-term goal, you may want to stay away from growth stocks. This is due to the fact that you are not likely to make much of a profit on a growth stock in the short term, and it is unlikely that you will see any return on the investment until you sell the stock. Step two is to evaluate the growth potential in the industry and company of the stock you are looking at. It is important here to check the economic condition of the industry. If the industry is in a recession, it is likely that the company will not be able to reach its growth potential. This is not to say that it is impossible to make a profit on a growth stock in a recession or depression, but the rate of potential is much higher during an economic boom. Finally, you will want to look into the past earnings performance of the company and the projected earnings. Make sure you know what you are buying and don't just take the company's word for it. Check other sources that provide information for stocks and make an informed decision.

*4.5. Dividend Investing*

Dividend stocks offer a higher yield rate with potential gains in stock value.

Often those in late stages of retirement move investment strategies to bonds with the intentions of living off interest money. This is a disadvantage because bonds only offer interest and are usually a lower risk and low return investment method. Bond interest rates plus yield rates on existing DM rating bonds are usually around 5-7% which offers little money when considering inflation rates. Bondholders can often be caught spending the interest knowing too late that they are now slowly eating away at the principal bonds.

Many people see it as a passive income method in retirement. The best part about this income is cash inflow from dividends is still considered part of capital and it can be reinvested to buy more shares of stock or to improve the quality of the portfolio. This is unlike interest income from bonds where the person would have to purchase bonds at a later date with lower coupon rates to earn the same amount of interest money.

So what exactly is so good about dividend investing and how is it different from value or purchasing a regular boring index. Well, in value investing, the person would invest in cheap companies and wait for the capital appreciation. With stock in dividends, the investor is still holding value, yet he is now being paid to hold the stock in his possession. An index with purchase power of $100,000 would now be worth $100,000 plus cash inflow from the dividends he receives on his stocks.

So exactly what is dividend investing? Investopedia defines it as: "A stock investment strategy that is based upon purchasing stocks that issue dividends. The investor selects stocks or a mutual fund that has a positive dividend track, aiming to receive the dividend as income, and also looking for potential capital appreciation."

So far we have learned 4 purchasing strategies, all aimed at increasing wealth. Dividend investing is another form of investing that deserves its own category as this investing style is becoming a top favorite with companies sitting on billions of dollars.

# CHAPTER 5

# Risk Management

Rebalancing is the task of adjusting your investment portfolio back to your target asset allocation. This is done by selling some of an asset that is overweighted in the portfolio or buying more of an asset that is underweighted in relation to the target asset mix. By doing this, you buy low and sell high, the opposite of what caused the original over/underweighting since assets at their all-time highest price relative to other assets are overweighted and those at their lowest price are underweighted. This effectively makes rebalancing a contrarian investing strategy. Rebalancing is necessary because various economic events and market movements cause the value of different investments to grow at different rates, so over time your portfolio becomes a different risk/return profile to what you originally intended.

Asset allocation involves finding the best mix of different types of investments to meet your specific financial goals while taking acceptable levels of risk. Stocks, bonds, and cash and equivalents are the three main asset classes, with real estate and commodities/currencies as alternative investments. Each of these asset classes has different levels of risk and return, so by choosing a mix of these that is suitable to your financial goals, you can effectively manage your risk. For example, if you are investing for retirement and you are currently age 40, you would generally be advised to have a portfolio consisting largely of stocks as you have a long time horizon until retirement and can therefore afford to take the high risk/high return option. On the other hand, if you are at retirement age, you want a low-risk investment to provide for you during your retired years, therefore you should allocate more of your investments into bonds and cash.

Diversifying your investment portfolio reduces the risk of poor performance from any one investment by spreading your money among many investments. If all of your money is in one stock and that stock fails, you will not be very happy. However, if that stock fails while the rest of your investments do well, the damage is much less.

*5.1. Diversification*

An example of diversification is a global superannuation investment fund. This fund generally invests in a mix of asset classes from equities and property to fixed interest and cash. The fund then subdivides and invests these asset classes in various global and Australian markets. This is similar to the investment strategy which I would use with an initial investment of $120,000. I would invest 60% or $72,000 in higher risk, high return investments, and 40% or $48,000 in low risk, low return investments. With reference to the investment simulation, the global superannuation investment fund diversified its aggressive and defensive investment asset allocations to maximize its overall expected return within a suitable risk level, and this is the same strategy which I want to use to diversify my $120,000 investment.

A diversified portfolio is one that contains a variety of different investments within a range of sectors. The basic idea behind this is that different investments will do well at different times, and many times there are investments that will underperform. Diversification can also add value to an investment strategy by exposure to a variety of different markets, whether it's the shares of a foreign country or small-cap stocks. Being diversified can benefit investors who don't put all their eggs in one basket and can be a safety net for an investment strategy. On the other hand, there is no point in diversifying an investment portfolio if it will not increase the expected return. It is expected that higher returns come with higher risks, and diversification is used to reduce risk. Although it is good to be a diversified investor, it is not smart to over-diversify. Over-diversification has nearly the same effect as not diversifying an investment strategy, as the proportion of the highest risk investment approaches the risk-free investment.

*5.2. Asset Allocation*

Asset allocation is the most important of the five concepts. It has been argued that the actual process of picking individual investments is not nearly as important as deciding what asset classes to include in a portfolio. Paul Kaplan, Ph.D., of Morningstar, provided evidence supporting this claim in a 2006 research paper. He created model portfolios and performed a multitude of simulations to determine the impact the asset allocation decision has on portfolio performance. Kaplan's findings allude to the notion that an investor should simply stuff a suitcase with the chosen asset class investment and go on vacation. While there may be a better way to reach their final destination, the selected choice will get the job done. This is to say that the specific investment vehicle and its returns are of little importance compared to staying within that asset class and systematically saving and investing. Since there are many arguments for the importance of asset allocation and the diverse range of evidence surrounding each argument, it is not clear whether it truly is the most important concept. What is clear, though, is that it is impossible to argue the impact asset allocation has on a portfolio and the risk-adjusted returns it attains. For this reason, this concept will have a significant influence on the writing which follows.

*5.3. Rebalancing*

Rebalancing is the most important and yet often overlooked aspect of the investment architecture. Most people go to great lengths to figure out the best asset allocation, and then forget all about it as they let their money simmer away in the market. After a year or two, they will have wildly different proportions of their money in the various asset classes depending on their relative investment performances. From an initial position of 60% stocks, 30% bonds, and 10% commodities, a successful year in the stock market could leave someone with 80% stocks, 12% bonds, and 8% commodities. These people will then experience the adverse of timeless investment advice of buying low and selling high. That is, after a successful year in the market, buying more stock is buying it at a higher price compared to the other investments, and having to sell off commodities to readjust their allocation is selling low relative to their purchase price. Essentially, they become victims of intermittent asset allocation without even realizing it and watching everything ride. A simple analogy is when oil traders experience tacit directional bets despite having a neutral opinion on the price because they buy high and sell low when the price is rising.

*5.4. Stop Loss Orders*

With every stop loss recommendation, it is important to remember to take the stop and not to go back on the decision. If the underlying conditions of the trade have changed and it is no longer valid, there is no shame in taking a loss.

A scaling stop is used for getting out of a trade which you are currently in the money on. It is a stop and reverse method which involves taking some of your position off and moving a stop loss order to a position where you believe the trade has become invalid. This is a difficult decision, but once you have taken money off the table, you will have demonstrated an objective view of the trade and taken into consideration any information which may affect the remaining portion of the trade. A stepping stop is a term used for changing the position of a stop loss order depending on how the trade progresses. This may involve moving the stop further as a position goes in your direction or nullifying the trade and exiting for minimal damage.

Emergency stop is a term used for a mental stop which you execute if the trade does not go the way you intended. You may decide it on a certain move against you, or a particular chart pattern which gives you a signal to exit the trade. If this stop is likely to be within an immediate price area, you may as well just place the actual stop order. It is a mistake to lose more in a trade than you had originally planned, so it's important to get out of a trade if it no longer meets the criteria which led you to take it on. A mechanical stop is a stop loss order and should be predetermined before you get into the trade. This kind of stop is less effective than, say, the emergency stop, as you are unlikely to want to exit the trade if it has become very profitable. However, it prevents massive losses and having determined a cut-off price which would confirm the trade idea is invalid, you would be able to assess the damage a losing trade can cause to your account.

Stop loss is a way to cut your losses quickly if the trade does not go in the direction you were hoping. It can be very effective in preventing large losses and can be used on all trades no matter what the time frame. There are different types of stops, but the basic premise of all is to get you out of a trade which you no longer want to be in. A stop loss order is an order to sell a stock at the market price when the stock reaches a predetermined price. Most investors are familiar with a stop order or stop loss order placed with their broker. If, and when, the stock trades at that price, the stop becomes a market order and the stock is sold.

*5.5. Hedging*

This is a very complex example, but it shows how an investor can use an option to offset future up or down stock price movements to try and guarantee a certain price at a given future date. This can be extremely useful for companies who are receiving a fixed payment in a foreign currency and wish to insure that they can get a certain amount of money in their home currency.

We can then keep the extra shares as well as the anticipated price increase for which we were not willing to risk. This overall will still be profitable even in the event that Microsoft shares fall from the current price.

This will leave us with the remaining option money to buy extra Microsoft shares. In either case above, we will want to sell the options at the new higher share price since this is 'in the money' and it is likely that we will exercise the options and buy the shares. This strategy has given us an extra $5000 to buy more shares in 3 months' time if the current share price is at or above the option strike price.

At this stage, we would then sell these options to a trader who is looking to buy Microsoft shares at $35 and simultaneously use the $500 profit to buy the shares at the new higher price. If the shares are at the same or a higher price than the option price in 3 months' time, and this is all we have done, then we will exercise the options and use the extra $5000 for our given example to reimburse the price difference on the shares $5000/(35-30) = 10 shares.

By doing this, we have secured the right to purchase $3000 worth of Microsoft shares per option contract at the current market price in 3 months' time. If the shares are above $30 in 3 months' time, the options will be 'in the money' and will be worth the price difference between the option and the share price x 100. i.e. if the share price is $35, then the option is worth (35-30) x 100 = $500.

We could buy the shares and then buy an 'at the money' (current price) 3-month expiry Microsoft Call option with a contract size of 100. Each option contract is worth $30 x 100 = $3000 Microsoft shares. So, one option contract is for 100/30 = 3.33 shares. As the options are only available in multiples of 100, we would buy 10 option contracts to equal the 1000 shares.

For example, let's say we are looking to purchase 1000 Microsoft shares currently at $30. We think that the market is going to move into an upward trend in the short term, so we want to buy these shares and profit from the increase. However, we are unsure of the long-term outlook and specifically the price of these shares in 3 months' time.

Hedging involves taking an offsetting position in a derivative in order to try and offset a potential loss/gain on the underlying. This technique is often used when the investor is unsure of the future price movement of a stock and wishes to insure their investment.

# CHAPTER 6

# Retirement Planning

A traditional 401(k) retirement account is an employer-sponsored plan where employees save and invest tax-deferred income. Usually, the contribution is directly taken out of your paycheck and put into the account. Some companies will match your contribution up to a certain percent. This is basically free money, and you should contribute at least enough to get the full matching amount. These plans are often the best retirement savings vehicle. Make sure to find out if your employer's 401(k) is a traditional type or more like the newer Safe Harbor 401(k). (A new Roth 401(k) is now available; we will discuss this further in the IRA section).

6.1.1 401(k)/Similar Plans

It's never too early or too late to start saving for your future. And our future depends on just how well we're prepared throughout our working career. There are several retirement savings accounts to choose from. How you use them depends on your needs, your desired lifestyle, and your employment situation. The best plan is often a combination of the 401(k) Plan, Regular IRA, and Roth IRA. From different employer-sponsored plans to the IRAs, find out which account is best for you and your family and how to get the most out of them.

6.1 Understanding Retirement Accounts

Retirement is not the end, but a new beginning. It is important to have a plan for the future for when you are ready to stop working and enjoy life. This chapter will help you prepare for your future. It will suggest ways to maximize your income when you retire, and also suggest ways to prepare for uncertainties and health concerns. Retirement planning is very important; it can be the difference between just getting by, and enjoying your life after your career.

## 6.1. Understanding Retirement Accounts

An Individual Retirement Account (IRA) is an account that allows you to save for your retirement and take advantage of tax benefits. There are myriad investment options available, including stocks, bonds, mutual funds, and ETFs. You are also able to save in the form of cash. You can hold an IRA account at a financial institution, such as a bank or a brokerage, or with a life insurance company. An IRA can be an effective retirement tool for many investors because of the flexibility it offers. With a traditional IRA, the money you contribute is generally tax-deductible, and any earnings can potentially grow tax-deferred until you withdraw them in retirement. The amount you pay in taxes and the tax benefits you receive will depend on your income level and whether you are covered by another retirement plan. During retirement, you may be in a lower tax bracket and may, therefore, enjoy a "tax savings" on the amount you withdraw, as it will be taxed at the lower rate. You also have the option of consolidating other retirement accounts into an IRA to facilitate managing your retirement savings. Simulation results are based on your input and some assumptions. Your results may vary with each use and over time.

Once you have a grasp of the various retirement accounts available, you can make better decisions on how to build your retirement nest egg. Generally, you're going to use a mix of retirement savings options to build your retirement savings. Your financial advisor can help you build a strategy that allocates your retirement savings into the various investment products in the most efficient manner. This Retirement Savings Planner is designed to provide a projection of what your approximate monthly income in retirement will be and whether or not this will meet your needs. The Planner helps you build, assess, and revise your retirement strategy not only before retirement begins but also while you are in retirement.

## 6.2. Calculating Retirement Needs

The final step requires knowledge of your current savings, the number of working years before retirement, and expected rates of return on investments. In this case, we will assume that there are $200,000 of current savings, 25 working years, and an average of 8 percent per annum on investments.

Next, determine the income/salary that you'll need to achieve a comfortable lifestyle. In this instance, it is $40,000 per annum. Multiplying this figure by 70 percent provides a target income of $28,000. High-income earners may adjust this figure to 75%, however, those on lower incomes may need to stay at 70 percent or even 65 percent.

Start with the age that you plan to retire. Subtract that from your estimated life expectancy to determine the number of years that you will need to fund retirement income. Many calculators use an average life expectancy; however, considering your health and family history may enable a better prediction. Subtracting 65 from 85 provides 20 years.

Sufficient annual retirement income. This section primarily focuses on the financial aspects of your retirement. It is recommended that you firstly calculate how much income you'll need to ensure a comfortable standard of living. Experts suggest that you'll need about 70 percent of your current annual income during each year of retirement. The lower your income, the higher a percent of your income you will need to maintain your standard of living. If you are in a low-income bracket and will need 90 percent of your income, the calculation can be adjusted to suit your needs. To calculate retirement needs that are based on saving a percent of your income to achieve a certain level of income during retirement, use the following easy steps that can be done on the back of a napkin or via a simple computer spreadsheet. Let's assume that you are age 40 and wish to determine how much you'll need to save in order to retire at age 65 and achieve an annual income of $40,000.

## 6.3. Maximizing Social Security Benefits

Social Security used to be a simple program. Retirement was at age 65 and the decision was whether to take early benefits at age 62 or delayed benefits which were higher. Spouses were typically of the same age, so coordinating benefits was also straightforward. Life expectancies were such that people usually did not get benefits for very long. They began at 65 and ended at 72. Social Security was a program to combat old-age poverty, and it worked well. Today, Social Security is still a foundation of retirement income. It has also become an extremely complex program with a variety of ways to claim benefits. Social Security planning is also an integral part of retirement planning. With an increasing number of baby boomers reaching retirement age, the role of Social Security as retirement income is a major concern for many people. This chapter will attempt to explain the basics of Social Security benefits and maximization of those benefits.

## 6.4. Creating a Retirement Income Strategy

A retirement income strategy is a plan for generating an income during retirement. It includes a detailed plan of working longer, saving more, and spending less during the years approaching retirement, and a plan for drawing down assets and a spending plan during retirement. This strategy utilizes the 3 fundamental methods to generate retirement income: employer pensions, government programs, and private savings and investment. Most of the retirement plans evolve from the preretirement stage to the postretirement. A retirement income strategy should be reviewed periodically and revised if necessary. An individual's circumstances and economic conditions are subject to change, and a good retirement income strategy should adapt to mitigating potential risks and uncertainty. These risks include the risk of outliving one's assets, the risk of unanticipated medical expenses, and the risk of increased living expenses. By establishing a wedge between investing and spending during the working years, an individual can accumulate enough wealth to comfortably maintain or increase living standards during retirement. Effective planning can ensure that an individual lives out their lives without financial worry and provides for heirs or charitable organizations.

## 6.5. Long-Term Care Planning

Long-term care refers to the ongoing services and support needed by people who have chronic health conditions that prevent them from doing everyday tasks on their own. There are many different pathways that long-term care can take, and it is important to plan and prepare for these situations. The U.S. Department of Health and Human Services estimates that 70% of people turning age 65 can expect to use some form of long-term care during their lives. The Aging, U.S. Census Bureau reports that over 40 million people are age 65+ in the United States, which accounts for 13% of the population. These numbers are increasing, and as the baby boomer generation has all turned 65 as of 2011, it is expected that the population age 65 and older will double between 2003 and 2030, which will increase the need for long-term care. When planning for retirement and long-term care, both are interconnected in terms of finances and quality of life. One of the primary goals associated with retirement planning is to make sure you don't outlive your income and assets. This means planning for an extra cushion of savings in the event that you may need to pay for long-term care due to a health condition. Long-term care can be very expensive, and the last thing you want to do is burden your family in having to support you. A long-term care situation may also involve a spouse, and it is important to consider what effect this may have on their quality of life. Depending on the severity of the situation, it may be necessary to be cared for in a nursing home or other facility. The goal is to try and maintain the highest level of independence and function for as long as possible. These are proper subject matters to address in an overall estate planning strategy.

# CHAPTER 7

# Tax Considerations

Minimizing costs is the key to tax-efficient investing. One of the best ways to reduce taxes is to simply buy and hold investments. This strategy will allow you to defer capital gains tax – the tax payable on any capital gains made from selling an investment. It's important to consider taxes when choosing which investments to hold in taxable accounts and which to hold in tax-advantaged accounts. Generally, investments that are less tax-efficient (i.e. they tend to generate a high amount of annual taxable income) should be held in tax-advantaged accounts in order to shelter the income from tax. This will allow you to keep the maximum amount of income generated from the investment and will allow the investment to grow at a faster rate. High-yield bonds and small-cap stock are examples of investments which are less tax efficient. It's common for investors to have US and international equities in taxable accounts as these investments are more tax-efficient.

By the time you begin to consider tax implications, you'll likely have a diversified portfolio of investments in various types of accounts. Determining the best way to invest in and withdraw from your various accounts will give you the best chance to minimize taxes and keep more of your money working for you. Above all else, remember, do not let the tax tail wag the investment dog. In other words, while it's important to consider tax implications, it's not worth making changes to your investment strategy that will cause you to incur more fees or take on more risk. This will inevitably cancel out any tax advantage.

*7.1. Tax-Efficient Investing*

Studies have shown that tax efficiency is more important than all other factors in producing after-tax returns. Tax efficient investing involves strategies to manage the impact taxes have on your investment returns. It, therefore, can be an essential factor in building wealth. The starting point for tax-efficient investing is to assess your current tax rate, take note of the fact it may well differ in the future, and then have an understanding of the tax implications of different types of investments. Typically speaking, interest income is taxed as ordinary income, and investments that generate this type of income are deemed to be less tax efficient. This is because if you have say a 30% marginal tax rate, a 5% bond yield will only return 3.5% after tax. Stepping up the tax efficiency ladder we come to qualified dividends and long-term capital gains which are taxed at rates of 15% for those in the 25-35% tax brackets, and 0% for those in the 10-15% brackets. Finally at the top of the tax efficiency ladder are investments that produce income tax free, such as municipal bonds and Roth IRAs. It is beneficial to have a mixture of these different types of investments to enable the highest after-tax return. This often means placing tax-inefficient investments inside of a qualified account.

*7.2. Capital Gains and Losses*

When you sell an investment or other property, the difference between the price you bought it for and the price for which you sell it is known as a capital gain or a capital loss. Capital loss occurs when the selling price is less than the purchase price. Short-term capital gains, on investments held less than one year, often result in tax being owed at the investor's regular tax bracket. Long-term capital gains and losses, on the other hand, are taxed at a lower rate, usually about 15% depending on the individual's tax bracket. High-income earners may also be subject to an additional 5% tax on long-term capital gains. This tax rate is a lot more favorable than that for interest on savings accounts or income from work. Any investment that produces these types of gains should therefore be very desirable, as is the case with tax-advantaged investments in retirement accounts. These investments are discussed in the next section and are deemed favorable because taxes on capital gains are deferred until the money is withdrawn from the account, and in the case of Roth IRAs, no tax is owed on the gains because contributions are made with after-tax dollars.

*7.3. Tax-Advantaged Accounts*

A tax-advantaged account is any type of investment, account, or plan that is either tax-deferred or tax-exempt. Tax advantaged is a financial product or account that is sheltered from taxes. A tax-advantaged situation or investment could mean any number of things: it could mean that capital gains taxes are lower in the account. It could mean that returns are only partially taxed. It could mean that tax is completely avoided. A tax-advantaged account allows you to earn an income and enjoy specific tax advantages. Earnings in your account generate a return and are considered growth. This growth is allowed to accumulate either tax-deferred or tax-free. In the former, that means that you won't have to pay taxes on the growth, but you will have to pay taxes on the principal contributions when you withdraw. In the latter, you won't have to pay any taxes at all on the growth or the principal. Common tax-advantaged accounts in the US are IRAs and 401(k)s, which provide an incentive for saving for retirement. Each of these accounts offers tax-free growth and tax-free principal withdrawal, allowing you to avoid paying any taxes. Other examples are college savings plans and health savings accounts, which provide tax-advantaged situations to save and spend on specific qualified expenses. With an educational savings plan, for example, you will not be taxed on any withdrawals that are used for qualified higher education expenses.

*7.4. Tax Planning Strategies*

The final strategy is to time your capital gains to occur when you are in the lower 15% income tax bracket. At these income levels, the tax on long term capital gains is 0%. By following Rule #1 investing principles you will not have to liquidate an investment at a bad time because you will always have a price for the best and a price for the worst. With this level of control, you can time when the investment no longer has significant ROI to sell and take the gains. Given proper planning and after building wealth, you will likely be able to manipulate when income occurs to stay in the desired tax bracket.

The tax exempt step is to purchase state-specific municipal bond funds. Interest from these securities is tax exempt when used to fund government projects. Do not purchase a national or international municipal bond fund because the income may still be subject to taxation (consult your tax professional to be certain). Also, do not purchase individual municipal bonds unless you purchase bonds specific to your home state. If you invest in bonds from other states, the interest is subject to federal taxes and often state taxes in that particular state.

I'm happy to report that the last three planning strategies really can save you money! First, if you are in the 10% or 15% income tax bracket and do not expect to move to a higher bracket in the near future, invest in securities that provide qualified dividends. Qualified dividends are taxed in the aforementioned brackets at 0%. The most common securities providing qualified dividends are common stocks.

*7.5. Working with a Tax Professional*

Once you have decided that a tax professional is right for you, finding the right one is the next step. If all you need is help with tax preparation, it may be as simple as walking into a local H&R Block. The cheapest and least desirable option is to go to one of the national tax chains. A much better and still very cost-effective option is to select an individual who has recently obtained a CPA or other tax professional certification but lacks experience. College business or accounting students often have the necessary knowledge for your situation but at a lower cost. The ideal is to find a tax professional that is experienced with your particular tax situation. For investment-related tax situations, the ideal is a CPA who is a Personal Financial Specialist or a tax attorney with an LLM in tax. High-income individuals with investments may find the tax services offered by a financial planner to be very helpful because it can be integrated with the individual's entire financial plan. A person with a complex business tax situation may need a tax attorney or CPA that specializes in that area. Assuming the tax professional is right for you, maintaining a good relationship with the individual for several years can be very beneficial. This often enables the professional to give better advice since it often takes a year to implement certain tax planning strategies and the professional will have a better understanding of your overall tax situation.

Deciding when to hire a tax pro and the type of professional you need are very important decisions. Not everyone needs a tax professional. If you have prepared your own tax return and have come up with creative ways to reduce your tax bill, then a tax professional may be able to save you even more money. Also, if your tax situation is very complex, whether because you are self-employed, run your own business, own foreign investments, or other reasons, hiring a tax professional is likely a good move. If your income is low and you have very few investments, you may only need a tax professional every few years, once you have him or her set up the proper tax planning strategies, discussed in section 7.4. If you are at or near retirement, a tax professional familiar with PF and/or retirement distributions can be very helpful.

# CHAPTER 8

# Monitoring and Adjusting Your Portfolio

It is a good idea to review and reassess your investments on a regular basis to make sure they are still meeting your investment goals.

Then you will need to make a note of the percentage and compare it to the percentage at a previous date. If the percentage has gone down, it is not a good sign. And if it has gone down a lot, it may be time to make adjustments to your portfolio.

You will need to keep a record of the number of each type of investment and what it is currently worth. Total up the value of each type of investment and compare this to the total amount of invested money. Then divide to get the percentage.

Tracking the performance of your investments is an important part of monitoring your portfolio. Just knowing the overall value of your investments is not enough. You need to know how each type of investment is performing compared to the others. If you use investment tracking software, you may be able to track your investments' performance as a whole. But if not, this can be a bit tricky to do.

*8.1. Tracking Performance*

If you have investments in funds with an investment strategy, you should be able to get a report from the fund manager on the relative performance of that fund with an explanation.

The first step in tracking performance is to be able to build a report on the performance of your investments. If you have an investment in an individual company, the process is simple - you need to keep a record of the fundamental results of that company. You should be wanting to keep periodic records of cash flow, profits, profit margins, and debt to equity in the form of a table. This data is publicly available in most countries. You then need to form an opinion regarding that investment. Ask yourself, was the original reason for the investment valid? Were there any changes in the company or economic conditions that you were unaware of? What was the relative strength of the company in comparison to the price of the investment? This process can be summarized with an expression of the investment's expected return.

The aim of tracking performance is to enable you to learn from your mistakes and successes. You should also be able to gain confidence in what you are doing and know when it is time to take action and when it is time to sit tight. It is important to devise a methodology that keeps you in touch with your investments and at the same time does not take up a large proportion of your time. Do not make the mistake of looking at your portfolio two or three times a day if you are a long-term investor. This can lead to overtrading and higher costs without additional benefits.

*8.2. Reviewing and Reassessing Investments*

A well-planned review and reassessment of your investment portfolio is fundamental to maintaining its health. We recommend a thorough review at least once a year and for some, especially those in or near retirement, every six months is better. This does not mean you should obsess over your investments every day as this is unnecessary and can be detrimental to your portfolio. A smart investor knows the fine line between proper maintenance and over managing. The purpose behind reviewing and reassessing a portfolio is ensuring it is still meeting your objectives and its overall asset allocation is still suitable. For many investments, especially those in managed funds, there is often a misalignment between the investment's original objective and the investor's current objective. For example, the investor's risk tolerance may have changed but the manager is still pursuing the fund's initial objective.

*8.3. Making Adjustments as Needed*

The most successful individual investors, institutional investors, and investment managers, all have one thing in common: they make investment decisions based on the best information available. That does not mean that they make all their decisions based on "inside information" or questionable market forecasts. It means that they have a process, a systematic way of obtaining the best information on which to base their investment decisions, and they do not deviate from this process. While nobody has a foolproof method for obtaining the best information, the most successful investors will all agree that following a process is better than making ad hoc decisions. With that in mind, let's consider a systematic approach to obtaining the best information for investment decision-making.

When building and maintaining a portfolio, you will need to make adjustments from time to time. The performance of investments will change and the asset allocation in your portfolio will deviate from your target as a result of these performance differences. For example, if one investment has outstanding performance, it may increase the percentage of your portfolio total comprised by that investment more than you originally intended. Ideally, you would like to sell off some of this investment, taking the profits and reinvesting the original sum without increasing your exposure to that investment. This would involve selling high, the opposite of what many investors do out of greed.

*8.4. Staying Informed about Market Trends*

The stock market may seem unpredictable, but certain factors can signal changes in the market and the economy. It is important to stay informed about general market trends if you are to be a successful investor. It is possible to make money in any kind of market, but an uptrend makes it a great deal easier. Any investor should know in which phase of the cycle the economy is. For example, investing in consumer durables in a recession would not be a good idea. Investors should be aware of what is happening in different sectors of the economy, i.e., technology, health, resources, etc. Political events have a big impact on the economy and financial markets. For example, the recent war in Iraq had a substantial impact on the price of oil and oil-related investments. Natural disasters can also have an impact. The recent devastating Australian bushfires and floods will have affected many local businesses and could impact certain investment sectors. Inflation or deflation causes changes in interest rates, which impact many investments. Always try to think through the implications of changing factors in the economy on your investments. For example, an interest rate change could have a very different impact on debt and equity investments.

*8.5. Seeking Professional Advice when Necessary*

A full-service broker provides clients with advice, recommendations, and a range of services including retirement planning, estate planning, tax tips, and wealth management. Stock brokers usually concentrate mainly on investing. He/she would obtain information on what you want to invest in and then use his knowledge of the market/investing to make recommendations and provide detailed instructions for investment decisions. He could also provide ongoing advice and monitor the progress of your investments. In both cases, the level of service and the fees involved will vary, so you should do some research to find what's best for you.

Financial planners can provide assistance on cash flow management to help you have the income for special events or purchases like education or travel. He/she can also give investment advice to help you reach your financial goals and set recommendations for an appropriate investment strategy. Normally, their guidance will involve taking a comprehensive look at your current financial situation and helping you to develop a detailed financial plan for the future. This could be a very focused plan or, in some cases, a comprehensive plan for your retirement years.

Seeking out professional advice is an important approach for new investors. There's a lot to learn even with the help of investment books, and it may be difficult to understand where to begin or how to apply an investment strategy. Furthermore, linking information to implementation can be hard, so professional help may prove to be useful. There are ways in which a person can seek professional advice. These include talking to a financial planner, talking to a stock broker, using a discount brokerage, and using an investment software package.

Milton Keynes UK
Ingram Content Group UK Ltd.
UKHW031400011224
451790UK00009B/135